A Guide to

Marie Kondo's

The Life-Changing Magic of Tidying Up:

The Japanese Art of

Decluttering and Organizing

Summary and Analysis,

Key Ideas and Facts

by

I.K. Mullins

Brief, Concise and to the Point
Publishing

A Guide to Marie Kondo's The Life-Changing
Magic of Tidying Up

A Guide to Marie Kondo's The Life-Changing
Magic of Tidying Up: The Japanese Art of
Decluttering and Organizing — Summary and
Analysis, Key Ideas and Facts

ISBN-13: 978-1511434782

ISBN-10: 1511434783

www.ideas-facts-books.com

Cover image credit: Zinaida Romanovskaya

Disclaimer

This is not the actual Marie Kondo's *The Life-Changing Magic of Tidying Up: The Japanese Art of Decluttering and Organizing*. The primary objective of this book is to bring insightful discussion and critique of Marie Kondo's *The Life-Changing Magic of Tidying Up: The Japanese Art of Decluttering and Organizing* to readers everywhere.

This book is not endorsed or affiliated with Marie Kondo, or any person or entity associated with Marie Kondo's book, *The Life-Changing Magic of Tidying Up: The Japanese Art of Decluttering and Organizing*. Do not purchase this BOOK if you are looking for a full copy of Marie Kondo's *The Life-Changing Magic of Tidying Up: The Japanese Art of Decluttering and Organizing*.

Table of Contents

Preface

Marie Kondo is a Japanese home-organizing guru and a consultant who specializes in tidying. In her book, *The Life-Changing Magic of Tidying Up*, Kondo explains her method of tidying up, offering valuable insights into clutter, its causes and its various types.

The Life-Changing Magic of Tidying Up is more than just another book about de-cluttering. It is an inspiring philosophy of letting go of the things that we do not need and keeping only the things that bring joy to our lives. Kondo's book has captured the attention of readers in many countries, helping them get rid of the burden of clutter and changing their lives with the clarity that comes from simplicity. The "tidying up" method developed by Kondo has already become part of popular culture. Many people already use her last name as a verb that describes purging things or folding them in a particular way.

A Guide to Marie Kondo's The Life-Changing Magic

of Tidying Up includes an unofficial summary of the key ideas and facts of Kondo's book, supplemented with analysis and comments on each key idea, as well as critical analysis of Kondo's principal messages.

Introduction

Marie Kondo, a Japanese home-organizing guru and a consultant specializing in tidying, has developed her own method of tidying up that has gained great popularity in many countries. In her book, *The Life-Changing Magic of Tidying Up*, Kondo tells how her life experiences and quest for tidiness allowed her to develop and perfect her tidying method, the KonMari Method.

Kondo grew up in Tokyo. From a young age, she became fascinated with cleaning and organizing living spaces. When Kondo was a child, she read home and lifestyle magazines. She even cleaned her siblings' bedrooms. When she was five years old, the Feng Shui space harmonization method became very popular in Japan. Kondo recalls how her mother applied the Feng Shui method to their home, but Kondo felt that it did not help to keep the home tidy enough.

At the age of 18, Kondo got a part-time job at a

Shinto shrine. Her job responsibilities required her to keep order for the shrine elder and to sell lucky charms at a kiosk. While in college, she studied sociology and wrote a thesis that was titled "'How to De-Clutter Your Apartment' — from a sociological perspective." When Kondo turned 19, she started a home-organizing consulting business when she realized that many of her clients had difficulty deciding what they should keep and what they needed to discard.

Kondo wrote her first book about tidying in just three months. The book was published it in 2010. It was initially intended for Kondo's clients who had signed up for her consulting services and were put on a months-long waiting list. However, in 2011, Japan was hit by an earthquake and tsunami. The catastrophe made people in Japan face important and profound questions. What things were essential in their lives? How valuable were their sentimental items? What was really most important about their lives? Consequently, Kondo's book gained great popularity in Japan, offering its readers a philosophy of letting things go.

In her book, Kondo points out that the majority of people have never had formal training on how to consistently clean and organize their living places. As a result, they live in apartments and houses that are full of clutter. The KonMari Method described in Kondo's book fills the gap in people's understanding of efficient tidying, enabling people to reform their own spaces both physically and mentally. It also gives people skills that can be readily transferred to other areas of their lives, including their work and relationships.

The KonMari Method does not allow any "escape routes" for keeping things that we do not need or do not like. According to this method, purging is to be done at once, without procrastination and without any "maybe" piles. Kondo advises her readers to keep only those things that make them happy and throw away or donate the rest. Once you get rid of clutter, she says, you will have a better idea of what you need in your home and your life.

Kondo emphasizes that her method goes beyond tidying up one's physical surroundings. It also helps people gain more clarity in their vision of life, personal priorities, likes and dislikes, hopes and dreams. Kondo believes that there is a connection between the state of a person's mind and the condition of their home, and that the process of tidying helps people gain new knowledge about their own mind and their life in general.

Considering how consumerism spreads around the world, it is no surprise that Kondo's book has become popular in many countries. Indeed, Americans and Western Europeans have experienced the growth of over-consumption for many years, and today developing countries are joining this trend. For example, in 1950, the average size of a new American home was 983 square feet, and an average of 3.37 people lived in each home. In 2011, the average new home in the US was 2,480 square feet, and the average number of people living in each home in the US decreased to 2.6 people.

Over the last 60 years, the amount of living space per capita in the US has increased by about three times. However, Americans do not seem to have enough space to store all their personal possessions. Their need for more storage space has spawned a more than 22 billion dollar personal storage industry in the US. Moreover, according to the Natural Resources Defense Council reports, about 40 percent of the food Americans buy goes into the trash.

Despite of what businesses promise their consumers, this endless consumption does not increase happiness. Subconsciously, we know the reason for that: happiness does not come from buying and having more stuff; real happiness comes from establishing good relationships, having meaningful jobs and fulfilling experiences, pursuing one's intellectual and spiritual interests. And this is what Kondo's book is about. Kondo reminds us that we do not need to fill our homes with material possessions in order to be happy. On the contrary, we can be happy with less stuff.

In my analysis of Kondo's book, I will review the main principles and the benefits of the KonMari Method. I will explore the findings of selected current psychological and sociological studies that address the relation between tidiness, mental health and happiness, and I will analyze how they compare to Kondo's ideas of tidiness, happiness and mindfulness.

In Part II of this book, I will also discuss how the KonMari Method misses one important step, which is crucial for those people who live in the countries where consumerism has established itself as the mainstream social and economic order and ideology. In my opinion, it is very likely that the followers of the KonMari Method who miss this step can relapse, returning to their old habit of over-consumption and over-stuffing their homes. I will further explain how you should be aware of the danger of such a relapse when you apply the KonMari Method to your life.

Part I. Summary and Analysis of Key Ideas in Marie Kondo's Book

1. The Essence of the KonMari Method

Marie Kondo's KonMari Method is based on a one-time event that has to occur within a relatively short interval (it might take up to six months). The event begins with a thorough sorting of all items in the home, followed by discarding of the items that do not make their owner happy. The event is concluded by choosing a place in the home for every item to be stored. Kondo proposes that the event of tidying will astonish and please its participants so much that they will completely give up their old clutter habits.

Kondo emphasizes that the KonMari Method is not just a set of rules on how to sort, discard, organize and store things; the method is designed to help people develop the right mindset for creating order in their homes for the rest of their lives.

A Guide to Marie Kondo's The Life-Changing Magic of Tidying Up

Kondo advises her readers to relinquish Feng Shui, flow planning and other methods of tidying and organizing. She proposes that people use the KonMari Method as a permanent solution to clutter and untidiness problems because it instructs people to keep only those items that bring joy in their lives. The ultimate goal of the KonMari Method is to increase happiness in people's lives by surrounding them with only those things that they need and that bring them joy. This is why people are motivated to use this method.

When people surround themselves only with objects that bring them joy, they have no difficulty discarding anything else. In other words, the KonMari Method requires people to choose what they want to *keep* in their homes instead of concentrating on what they have to discard. The KonMari Method also requires that people never keep objects simply because of their attachment to the past or future.

For those who are thinking about using the KonMari Method, Kondo says to ignore the advice about tidying in increments for, say, 15 minutes per day. You have to set aside some extended time and tackle everything over that period of time, and you have to start this process as soon as possible.

According to Kondo, this method can be applied to other areas of people's lives, including their relationships, beliefs and values.

Analysis and comments on the essence of the KonMari Method

The KonMari Method calls for a rapid one-time de-cluttering and organizing event that has to be completed systematically in no more than six months. To a certain degree, the KonMari Method is effective because it requires that instead of de-cluttering room by room, people first have to categorize items and then decide which items they want to keep. Kondo recommends beginning with clothes, then books and documents, followed by the items that belong to other categories. Finally, they have to deal with photos and other things of sentimental value.

In a way, the KonMari Method is related to the concept of minimalism, which is trending in the US *and Europe.* This concept implies that people should live with only those things that they most value and really need. The concept of minimalism opposes the mainstream modern culture, which is based on a belief that the good and enjoyable life can be found in buying things and having as many things as possible.

People, who subscribe to this mainstream cultural value of consumption, tend to expect that they can buy happiness at a department store. People, who advocate minimalism, argue that it frees people from the ever-growing desire for and therefore burden of having more and more material possessions. Minimalism encourages people to give up consumerism and seek happiness in relationships, life experiences and soul-searching.

The KonMari Method is supposed to be a one-time de-cluttering event. However, there is no real proof that it can reform people's mentality permanently. It is doubtful that a few months of categorizing and purging things can transform a long-term shopaholic or hoarder into a minimalist. After all, businesses spend huge money on marketing, bombarding people with messages about being happy while acquiring things. Marketers use findings from psychological and sociological studies in order manipulate people's conscious and subconscious thinking and make them acquire more things. Can the KonMari Method really stand up against them? I will discuss this further in Part II of my book.

2. Reasons for Clutter

According to Kondo, people have problems with tidying up when they are unable to discard some of their possessions, and when they fail to assign proper places for storing items that they own and/or put things back where they belong. In many cases, these issues can be easily resolved. However, Kondo observes in her book that some people have difficulty discarding things because of more serious psychological issues.

For example, some people have their homes full of clutter because they are over-attached to the past or the future. Such people are reluctant to let go some of their material possessions because they believe that they might need those items in the future. This kind of fear reflects people's anxiety about the future. In some cases, people have difficulty letting go of items that have some sentimental value. This is a sign that those people are clinging to the past.

Kondo emphasizes that when people with such

psychological issues want to de-clutter their homes, they have to address their attachment to the past or the future.

Analysis and comments on reasons for clutter

According to the KonMari Method, people should keep only those items in their homes that spark joy in their lives. Kondo found from working with her clients that some people do not discard certain items even though those items do not spark joy.

In her book, Kondo goes beyond the discussion of organizing material possessions and points out that people can learn a lot about themselves by analyzing their attachment to certain objects. She addresses some psychological issues that might cause clutter and validate people's hoarding behavior. Namely, she talks about people's attachment to the past and anxiety about the future. She also rightfully notices that people sometimes keep their relationships and jobs for the same reasons as they keep things that they no longer use.

A Guide to Marie Kondo's The Life-Changing Magic of Tidying Up

I would like to point out that the psychological issues that Kondo discusses in her book are not the only ones that can make it difficult for people to de-clutter. I review other psychological and psychiatric conditions that can promote clutter in Part II of my book.

Sometimes, those things that we cannot throw away tell us something about our subconscious desires and inspirations. For example, Jennifer Baumgartner, an American psychologist who authored the book titled *You Are What You Wear*, writes, "Our closets are windows into our internal selves. Say you're holding on to your team uniforms from college. Ask yourself, what about that experience did you like? What can you do in your life now to recapture that?" This messages correlated with Kondo's ideas about connections between the things we have and our dreams and memories.

Interestingly, some people can let things go very easily. Such people view themselves as very neat and organized. However, they often keep their place neat and "empty" by placing the burden of having and storing things on other people, including their friends and close relatives. There is a chance that you might have a close relative or a friend who boasts of his or her life with as few items as possible, but who frequently borrows basic things from you or somebody else.

Unlike "neatness extremists," some people feel inspired when they are surrounded by certain amount of clutter and mess. They view a clean desk as a sign of lack of thoughts and ideas. Empty desks make them feel like no work is being undertaken. Drastic cleaning and de-cluttering of their working space can do more harm than good to their work.

However, having "busy" desks is different from being subjected to informational clutter, which should be avoided by anyone as much as it is possible. Informational clutter includes any useless data stored on your computer, endless messages from Twitter, Facebook and other social sites, and other information that does not improve your life in any profound way. Both informational clutter and physical clutter can force you to lose your focus, make you less productive, and reduce joy in your life.

3. Psychological and Other Benefits of Decluttering and Tidying up

Kondo views the process of tidying as a conversation in which every item that doesn't "spark joy" has to be touched, thanked and sent to some place where it can find a new owner. By sending things off in such a thoughtful way, Kondo's clients and followers clean their homes from those items that carry the baggage of the past and/or those items that re-enforce their anxiety about the future. Consequently, they find themselves surrounded only by those things that give them mental clarity and joy.

When the clutter is gone, a person can examine his or her state of mind and realize what he or she really wants from life. According to Kondo, many people who have followed the KonMari Method have changed their lives in profound way. In her book, Kondo writes, "Keep only those things that speak to your heart. Then take the plunge and discard all the rest. By doing this, you can reset your life and embark on a new lifestyle."

Kondo emphasizes the emotional and psychological impact that cleaning can have on your life. She also mentions that one of the important objectives for cleaning your home is simply to feel happy living in your home. Another benefit of de-cluttering and organizing your home is to begin a brand new life and to apply the skills, which you have learned when tidying your home, to other areas in your life. This is what Kondo considers the magic of tidying.

Kondo proposes that once you learn to keep only those possessions that bring joy to your life, you will be able to apply the KonMari Method to other areas in your life, discarding whatever you keep just out of obligation. For example, Kondo suggests that tidying your home can help you find the right career or a relationship that can make you happy. She argues that people can improve their decision-making skills when they use the KonMari Method and decide which items to keep and which items to discard. Kondo also proposes that the process of tidying can help people lose weight.

Analysis and comments on benefits of decluttering and tidying up

Kondo's promises, which are described above, sound very interesting. However, they have been supported so far only by anecdotal stories of those transformations that have been experienced by her own clientele. Scholars and academic researchers might think that this is not a sufficient proof for her statements. Some people also might feel a bit put off by Kondo's advice to greet houses and to talk to their possessions as if they had feelings.

Nevertheless, Kondo's belief that tidying is important for mindfulness agrees with many psychological studies. I think that her idea of a relation between tidiness and mindfulness is well supported by studies conducted by Stephanie McMains and Sabine Kastner of Princeton University. Their studies provide new support for the view that a cluttered environment decreases people's ability to focus.

However, other studies conducted by Kathleen Vohs and her colleagues from the University of Minnesota indicate that a messy desk may promote creative thinking and stimulate new ideas. These researchers conducted experiments that found that being in a clean room may encourage people to do what they are expected to do. The participants of their experiments who were placed in a clean room generated as many ideas as the participants placed in a messy room. However, unbiased judges found that ideas generated by people located in the messy room were more interesting and creative than the ideas generated by the participants located in the clean room.

Vohs also proposes that a disorganized environment can inspire people to break free of tradition and find new insights, while a clean and organized environment encourages people to act in accordance with convention and play it safe. (Interestingly, Steve Job's office used to be rather cluttered—you can "google" photos of his office.)

My point is that the KonMari Method and tidiness may not meet all our expectations for quality of life. If you wish to stay focused and feel less stressed, then tidy environments created in accordance with the KonMari Method can help you with that. However, tidiness can block your creativity as well.

4. The Art of Visualization

Kondo advises that before you begin discarding any items from your home, you should visualize your ideal home and ask yourself what you would like to see in your home. If you need inspiration, you should take a look at interior decorating magazines or even visit model homes. You should also ask yourself how you would like to feel in your ideal home. Your vision should be concrete and specific. Its objective is to prepare you mentally and emotionally for identifying those items that bring joy to your life and discarding the items that do not bring joy. Your vision of the ideal home will help you get in touch with that feeling of joy.

A Guide to Marie Kondo's The Life-Changing Magic of Tidying Up

Analysis and comments on the art of visualization

Visualization has become a very popular personal development technique since the late 1970s. However, humans have actually been using this technique for millennia.

A visualization technique involves using our imagination to create visions of what we want in our lives as well as how we can realize our vision for a better life. When you imagine and mentally rehearse an event, your thoughts stimulate your nervous system. As a result, your brain creates the neural patterns that are needed for actions, which can bring about the desired outcome.

For example, in competitive sports, many coaches consider sports to be 90 percent mental and 10 percent physical. Many professional athletes learn and practice visualization (mental imagery). They do a complete mental run through the essential elements of their routines. Visualization helps athletes to focus and eliminate some pre-performance anxieties. As a result, they feel more comfortable and confident when they have to compete in real settings. It also serves as a warm-up or mini-rehearsal.

You can use the same kind of mental rehearsal in order to prepare yourself for a major tidying event. Visualization will help you focus, stay motivated and be confident in your ability to achieve your goals.

5. Sorting and Discarding

According to the KonMari Method, you have to de-clutter your home by category of item. The room-by-room de-cluttering does not work because people frequently store the same type of item in more than one room.

Kondo says that there are a few basic categories of items that you have in your home, and you have to deal with these categories in the following order:

1. clothing
2. books
3. papers
4. *komono,* or small items, such as DVDs and beauty products
5. sentimental items, including photographs and personal letters

In order to sort and discard items by category, you have to gather all the items that belong to the same category in one central location in your home. (Kondo recommends doing this in the morning.)

Then, you have to pick up each item, hold it in your hands, think about its meaning to you, and answer Kondo's question: Does it *tokimeku*—spark joy?

Kondo advises her readers, "Keep only the things that speak to your heart. Then take the plunge and discard all the rest." She further advises readers to thank their clothes for their service—or for teaching them something about their style and fashion mistakes—before sending them away.

In this process, as I discussed earlier, Kondo brings up the importance of analyzing the mental and emotional reasons for your attachment to certain things. Kondo emphasizes that you will find it easier to discard items once you realize that you are keeping them because of your attachment to the past or your anxiety about the future (sometimes it can be combination of both). She further points out that you have to become aware of your ownership pattern because it corresponds to the values that guide you in your life. In other words, your possessions can tell you how you want to live your life, and, by addressing those possessions that you do not need, you also confront your mental errors and psychological issues.

Kondo writes, "The best way to find out what we really need is to get rid of what we don't." She warns against putting any item away until you have completed the process of discarding. By putting items "on hold" (to decide later if you need them), you will jeopardize the de-cluttering process.

Clothing

According to Kondo, you have to gather all your clothing items and place them in the same spot. Clothing, shoes and accessories have to be sorted in the following order: tops, bottoms, clothes that should be hung, socks, underwear, handbags, accessories, clothes for specific events, shoes.

For each item, ask yourself if it causes a spark of joy—a quick feeling of happiness. If an item does not spark joy, then you have to discard it. To make the discarding process easier on you, you can start with off-season clothing and tell yourself that you choose what you intend to keep, not what you plan to give away.

Kondo speaks against downgrading clothes to loungewear. If you have any clothes that cannot be worn outside, then you should discard them. Also, if you feel very passionate about your clothing and think that it will be very difficult for you to decide which clothing items to keep, then you should begin the discarding process with another category of items.

Books

Kondo recommends her readers to place all books on the floor at one chosen location and decide which books spark joy. Those are the books that they will keep. If they have any unread books, they might be inclined to think that they will read them some time in the future. However, in this case, "sometime" almost certainly stands for "never." It is also unlikely that they will re-read books they have read and liked. So, people should donate the books that they do not plan to read and keep those books that they feel excited to read.

Papers

The paper category does not include papers that have sentimental value. According to Kondo, you should keep only those papers that require your action and those papers that must be kept permanently (e.g., a birth certificate), and you have to throw other papers away. Kondo argues that papers will never spark joy, they will only annoy you. Remember to shred credit card statements and other papers with sensitive identifying information.

Komono

Komono is a Japanese word that stands for "miscellaneous items," such as spare buttons, free samples, unidentified cords, etc. Kondo strongly advises you to get rid of them.

Sentimental items

Kondo emphasizes that sentimental items have to be the last items to sort and discard because you need to improve your ability to identify joy-sparking items before you get to the objects of sentimental value. She argues, for example, that keeping love letters from the past can weigh you down. Letters have to be discarded, photographs have to be sorted, and many photographs should be discarded as well. Do not keep gifts out of guilt. Donate them. Recycle electronics packaging and manuals. You can always find answers to your questions about electronics on the internet.

Also, in agreement with common sense, those items that are broken or out of date should be discarded.

Analysis and comments on sorting and discarding

Instead of tidying your home room by room, Kondo tells you to sort your possessions by category and then work with each category separately. This will save you time, considering that items from the same category can be stored in different rooms. Also, when you gather all the items from the same category in one place, you will get a better idea about the number of such items. You might discover that you have too many things in some particular category.

Kondo's plan for de-cluttering is unquestionably simple, which is a nice change for people who have to deal with complex situations at work and in their social lives.

Certainly, there are tricks that can help you with de-cluttering. For example, you should try to find a second home for those items that you wish to discard. Then, you will feel less separation anxiety and experience less guilt over being wasteful.

Kondo's advice to begin sorting and discarding with clothing agrees with what Jennifer

Baumgartner writes in in her book *You Are What You Wear*: "If you want to move forward, release the past, starting with your closet." You should apply the 80/20 rule to your clothing: most people wear about 20 percent of their clothing 80 percent of the time. You have to recognize those clothing items that reflects past sizes, past self-perceptions and past life roles. Obviously, these items should not be kept at your home.

6. Your Tidiness and Your Family

Kondo warns readers against secretly throwing away other family members' possessions. However, she does not recommend broadcasting to your family all the details of the purging process. This is why, in her opinion, you should first sort and discard your own things and "leave communal spaces to the end." According to Kondo, you should keep family members away from home while you are tidying. Otherwise, they will interfere and try to prevent you from getting rid of various items.

In her book, Kondo also talks about adult children who do not get rid of some items, but send them to their parents' homes, and younger siblings who receive lots of hand-me-down clothes.

Analysis and comments on your tidiness and your family

From her consulting experience, Kondo concludes that family members can obstruct your tidying plans. Therefore, you should ignore them and focus on your own stuff. It is difficult to discard items of sentimental value, and your family members with their emotional bonds and common past experiences can make it even more difficult, which is why they should not be involved in the tidying process.

Kondo believes that once your family members see how your tidying process improves your life, they will be more inspired and willing to change their own attitudes toward clutter and start their own tidying process.

7. Storing Your Possessions and Taking Care of Them

In her book, Kondo explains that after you discard every item that you do not wish to keep anymore, you have to designate a spot for every item that is left. Once you do that, your home will be full of items that bring you joy, and each item will be in its proper place. Kondo warns that, if you don't assign a designated place for each item, then your home will become cluttered again. Moreover, if you share your home with your family, then you must allocate separate storage spaces for each family member.

Kondo speaks against any fancy and sophisticated storage units. She considers them worthless and unhelpful for the most part, because they attract clutter. Many storage experts focus on filling complicated storage units with as many things as they can, without asking if these items can bring joy. Kondo says that the most common storage item she uses is an empty shoebox.

When it comes to papers, you have to have contracts (work-related, mortgage, etc.), as well as insurance policies, stored in an upright holder in order to avoid your "paper collection" getting too big.

According to Kondo, you have to learn how to fold clothes and store them "vertically." She points out that, with the exception of heavy cloth items, most clothing items are better kept folded than hung. Kondo claims that in the same amount of space you can store more folded clothing than hanging clothing. (You can find Kondo's folding videos on her YouTube site.) When you place your folded clothes, you must allow the folded clothes to "breathe" by standing them upright (at the height of the drawer).

Kondo points out that storage should minimize the effort that you make to put things away. According to Kondo, your items should be stored mostly in drawers, where they are arranged in such a way that you can see everything at a glance.

Kondo insists that no items should be stacked. You have to roll and arrange your T-shirts and socks in a visually pleasant way. You have to hang up those clothes that look "happier" hung up. For those people who carry handbags, Kondo recommends cleaning out a handbag every day and letting it rest while at home.

According to Kondo, it is important that you unpack all new items and remove labels from them before putting the new items away. You should not store any items close to the tub or sink where they can easily get messy. Most importantly, you have to learn to appreciate your possessions, thank them, and treat them with care. Those items that you do not want or do not use have to leave your home. And before they do, you have to express your gratitude to them. Kondo thinks that this will give you mental clarity that will lead to better relationships and better career paths. Once you learn what you really enjoy, you will be less willing to settle for something that you do not enjoy or enjoy less.

Analysis and comments on storing and taking care of your possessions

Kondo has a tendency to personify objects as if they were conscious. For example, when she talks about arranging similar items of clothing together, she comments that "Clothes, like people, can relax more freely when in the company of others who are very similar in type." The benefit of such an attitude might be that it will make you more inclined to take good care of them.

Whereas some people might feel uncomfortable with this kind of anthropomorphism, it is not a rarity in Japanese culture. The art of folding clothes is also very important in Japanese culture, particularly because of limited living space. People might find it challenging to follow Kondo's ideas of storing folded items vertically.

I am not certain why Kondo does not recommend using electronic devices, such as Kindle and iPad, for storing and reading digital editions of books. Today, many people can afford to have their own digital libraries that will not clutter their homes.

Part II. Critical Analysis of the Principal Messages of Kondo's Book

A Guide to Marie Kondo's The Life-Changing
Magic of Tidying Up

The KonMari Method is a unique decluttering and organizing method that includes two important activities:

- Identifying those possessions of yours that do not "spark joy" in you, thanking them for their service and discarding them;
- Designating a place for each item that you choose to keep in your home without buying any complicated organizing equipment.

According to Kondo, the process of discarding is a very intuitive process that can be learned. Those readers who feel positive about applying their intuition to a decision-making process should feel enthusiastic about the way in which the KonMari Method relies on intuition. On the other hand, those readers who value logic and rational thinking over intuitive thinking might find it difficult to use the joy-sparking approach.

Kondo writes about her KonMari Method with great conviction. She states that the KonMari Method is a universal method of tidying that will work for lots of different people. She further assures us that people who use the KonMari Method to declutter and organize their homes properly, will never need to battle clutter in their homes again. These two statements are debatable.

First, the KonMari Method is based on what Kondo has learned from her own history of trying out various techniques and programs, testing different storage solutions. Her conclusions about the effectiveness of the KonMari Method come from case stories of her clients—mostly female professionals and homemakers. We do not have sufficient information about its effectiveness for people of other age groups and gender.

Second, Kondo says in her book, "I can't claim that all my students have perfected the art of tidying. Unfortunately, some had to stop for one reason or another before completing the course. And some quit because they expected me to do the work for them." Therefore, some people do fail in their attempts to follow the KonMari Method, but no information is provided in her book or her later presentations on what percent of the total number of Kondo's students actually quit their training or what their reasons are for quitting.

Third, the KonMari Method was developed only

a few years before Kondo wrote her book, and no serious scientific studies have been conducted in order to verify that all the people who apply this method to their lives never go back to their original state of clutter.

Fourth, Kondo's proposal that the KonMari Method can be universally effective for people from different countries and cultures is questionable. It is certainly questionable with regard to American and Western European cultures, where the KonMari Method, which promotes minimalism, clashes with the culture of over-consumption and the mainstream belief that buying more things can make people feel happy.

From a very young age, people in the US and Europe are continuously subjected to marketing messages about having a spark of joy when they acquire material possessions. Consequently, it is difficult (and sometimes even impossible) for them to distinguish a spark of joy that they have when an item makes emotional connections with their true inner nature from a spark of joy that they get because they have been conditioned (programmed) by the marketing industry to experience joy from acquiring material possessions.

The KonMari Method does not help people to distinguish these two kinds of joy, and Kondo does not address this problem in her book. She does not suggest any meaningful way for her followers to develop awareness of how marketing techniques affect their psychology, defining their ability to experience joy from buying things and cluttering up their homes.

In some cases, informal social expectations and biases can play a role in addition to planned marketing manipulation. For example, a person can experience a spark of joy when buying an item that "plays along" with the person's vanity or when the item allows the person to create the appearance of achieving certain social status. These motives will not make the person happier over time, but the person will nevertheless experience a spark of joy from possessing those items and holding them in his or her hands.

Kondo writes that the things that people own are the consequences of the choices that they make, and by discarding objects indiscriminately, people are denying responsibility for the choices they make. Unfortunately, Kondo does not discusses how our social and economic systems affect these choices—to over-consume, buy things that are not needed and clutter our homes. The KonMari Method does not address the fact that the mainstream culture of over-consumption is the reason for cluttering in many cases.

Moreover, Kondo makes one statement in her book that I think is particularly worrisome when it comes to consumption-obsessed societies:

> Slimming belts, glass bottles for making kefir, a special blender for making tofu, a weight-loss machine that mimics the movement of horseback riding—it seems a waste to get rid of expensive items like these that you bought by mail order but never fully used. Believe me, I can relate. But **you can let them go. The exhilaration you felt when you bought them is what counts. Express your appreciation for their contribution to your life**

**by telling them, "Thank you
for the boost you gave me
when I bought you."**

That is, instead of advising people to remember
such unfortunate buying experiences next time
when they think to buy things they do not need,
Kondo tells people that they have to be thankful for
the boost that they get and the exhilaration that they
feel when they buy things that they do not need.

Such an approach can throw some people into a
repeating cycle of feeling liberated and renewed
when throwing things away and then, a few months
or a few years later, feeling exhilarated when
buying other things that they do not need (you can
always throw those things away later, thanking
them for giving you the thrill of buying them). In
this way, the KonMari Method can actually
encourage consumerism and wasteful over-
consumption supported by the economic system
that perpetually sends people messages about how
things can make them happy.

These considerations do not mean that I suggest
dismissing the KonMari Method as totally wrong or
ineffective. On the contrary, the KonMari Method

provides a clear strategy for de-cluttering, simplifying and organizing your life in order to make it more meaningful and enjoyable. However, it misses one important step that, in my opinion, has to be included in order for it to be really effective and to prevent people from a relapse. By relapse, I mean not just cluttering your place again, but buying things that you do not need.

The missing step is the principle of *mindfully* acquiring things in the first place, which requires you to explore the real reasons behind your purchases (for example, when you decide to discard things) and refuse to buy things out of vanity, because of social pressure and under the influence of marketing messages. Moreover, you have to educate yourself about the techniques that the economic system uses to lure people into buying things and make them think that buying more things is a way to joy and happiness.

For example, when you de-clutter your house and make a decision about discarding some of your possessions, ask yourself if they caused a spark of joy in you because of some marketing tricks. Ask yourself if those items sparked your life with joy because you really liked them or because they appealed to your vanity, or your desire to keep up or elevate your social status.

The principle of mindful acquisition requires us to realize, for example, that social status cannot be elevated through things. If a person lacks cultural and intellectual refinement, then buying things only gives that person an illusion of elevating his or her social status. Jean-Baptiste Poquelin, a French play writer and actor who is known by his stage name Molière, criticized this phenomenon in his play, *Le Bourgeois gentilhomme* (*The Bourgeois Gentleman* or *The Middle-Class Aristocrat*).

The principle of mindful acquisition also requires people to educate themselves about various tactics used by marketers. After all, according to the ReportLinker, the global management and marketing consultancy industry is expected to reach almost 388 billion dollars in 2015! This includes the money that businesses are willing to spend in order to manipulate consumers' minds, making them buying more things.

In our age of 24-hour online shopping opportunities, people with various socioeconomic statuses indulge themselves in buying products that they often do not need and that do not make them any happier. In stores, marketing specialists set numerous "traps" for customers, manipulating them into buying things as well. For example, in their article, "The Power of Touch: An Examination of Effect of Duration of Physical Contact on the Valuation of Objects," James Wolf, Hal Arkes and Waleed Muhanna point out that touching an item can make you become emotionally attached to it.

In their experiments, researchers asked participants to touch and examine coffee mugs. Then the participants were asked to participate in a sale where the mugs were auctioned off. It turned out that participants who held the mugs in their hands longer were ready to pay over 60 percent more for those mugs than participants who held the mugs in their hands for shorter periods. For example, Apple uses the psychological effect of touch in Apple stores, where you can touch and play with Apple products as if they were your own.

You will need to make a serious mental effort to free your mind from the influence of these numerous marketing techniques. This is why the principle of mindful acquisition is very important to any person who wishes to avoid cluttering his or her home with unwanted things.

In her book, Kondo explores how people's attachment to the past and their fears about the future relate to the choices they make when they decide which items to keep in their homes. However, the psychological issues that some people exhibit with respect to their past and their future are not the only ones that can lead to clutter. In fact, there many psychological and psychiatric conditions that can cause clutter in people's homes.

For example, some people have difficulty letting go of their things because they suffer with perfectionism, procrastination, separation anxiety, compulsive buying disorder, or issues with their physical appearance. In some cases, chronic disorganization and clutter can be a symptom of Obsessive-Compulsive Disorder, Attention Deficit Hyperactivity Disorder, and dementia.

Recently, psychiatrists identified a new type of psychiatric disorder—hoarding disorder—that is defined as "persistent difficulty discarding possessions, regardless of their value." Psychiatrists

estimate that about 2 to 5 percent of population may
have hoarding disorder. David Tolin and other
researchers from the Yale School of Medicine
studied two areas of the brain in people who are
predisposed to hoarding—the anterior cingulate
cortex and insula. The activity of these areas of
human brain is usually associated with physical
pain. The study demonstrated that these two areas
in brains of hoarders become activated when the
hoarders discard items that they own and cherish.
This means that a hoarder's brain perceives the loss
of possessions as an event that causes physical pain.

People with the conditions listed above have
difficulty with concentrating, planning, and making
decisions, and they remain in the states of denial,
anxiety and guilt as long as their psychological
issues are unresolved. It is highly unlikely that a
one-time de-cluttering event can cure their minds.
However, when applying the KonMari Method,
they may come to realization that they need
professional help to address their psychological or
psychiatric problems.

In most cases, though, clutter is not a result of
some psychiatric disorder, but it is a consequence of

less intransigent mental errors and flawed judgment; for example, when a person thinks that he or she should keep clothing of a wrong size just because one day he or she might lose weight and wear it.

Anybody can make mental errors. When you assess your material possessions, you can take the opportunity to recognize those patterns of irrational thinking and get rid of them, along with the things that you do not need.

* * *

I believe that the KonMari Method can improve the lives of many people when it is combined with the principle of mindful acquisition and acute awareness of social and marketing pressure that makes people buy things they do not need or really enjoy.

At the same time, I would like to point out that the idea of intuitive de-cluttering is not a new one. The idea of keeping only what you need and what gives you joy has been known in Western culture for a long time. For example, Henry David Thoreau, the early 19th century American naturalist, philosopher and author, conducted a two-year experiment living a simple life on the shores of Walden Pond (Massachusetts). He promoted simple and sustainable living in his book *Walden* (1854).

While modern Western culture welcomes thoughtful and enlightening words of wisdom from Marie Kondo, a Japanese organizing guru, I would like to remind you how more than hundred years ago, Jerome K. Jerome, a British writer, brilliantly described the idea of de-cluttering and simplifying in his book, *Three Men in a Boat: To Say Nothing of the Dog*:

> I call that downright wisdom, not merely as regards the present case, but with reference to our trip up the river of life, generally. How many people, on that voyage, load up the boat till it is ever in danger of swamping with a store of foolish things which they think essential to the pleasure and comfort of the trip, but which are really only

useless lumber.

How they pile the poor little craft mast-high with fine clothes and big houses; with useless servants, and a host of swell friends that do not care twopence for them, and that they do not care three ha'pence for; with expensive entertainments that nobody enjoys, with formalities and fashions, with pretense and ostentation, and with – oh, heaviest, maddest lumber of all! – the dread of what will my neighbour think, with luxuries that only cloy, with pleasures that bore, with empty show that, like the criminal's iron crown of yore, makes to bleed and swoon the aching head that wears it!

It is lumber, man – all lumber! Throw it overboard. It

makes the boat so heavy to pull, you nearly faint at the oars. It makes it so cumbersome and dangerous to manage, you never know a moment's freedom from anxiety and care, never gain a moment's rest for dreamy laziness – no time to watch the windy shadows skimming lightly o'er the shallows, or the glittering sunbeams flitting in and out among the ripples, or the great trees by the margin looking down at their own image, or the woods all green and golden, or the lilies white and yellow, or the sombre-waving rushes, or the sedges, or the orchids, or the blue forget-me-nots.

Throw the lumber over, man! Let your boat of life be light, packed with only what you need – a homely home and simple pleasures, one or two friends, worth the name, someone to love and someone to love you, a cat, a dog, and a pipe or two, enough to eat and enough to wear, and a little more than enough to drink; for thirst is a dangerous thing.

You will find the boat easier to pull then, and it will not be so liable to upset, and it will not matter so much if it does upset; good, plain merchandise will stand water. You will have time to think as well as to work. Time to drink in life's sunshine – time to listen to the Aeolian music that the wind of God draws from the human heart-strings around us...

References

Barber B. 2008. *Consumed: How Markets Corrupt
Children, Infantilize Adults, and Swallow Citizens
Whole*. W. W. Norton & Company

Baumgartner, J. 2012. *You Are What You Wear:
What Your Clothes Reveal About You*. Da Capo
Lifelong Books

Doland, E. "Scientists find physical clutter
negatively affects your ability to focus, process
information." 2011. Available at:
https://unclutterer.com/2011/03/29/scientists-find-
physical-clutter-negatively-affects-your-ability-to-
focus-process-information/

Frost, R. "Course and Causes of Hoarding."
Available at http://hoarding.iocdf.org/causes.aspx

James R. Wolf, J.R., Arkes, H.R., Muhanna, W. "The power of touch: An examination of the effect of duration of physical contact on the valuation of objects," 2008. Available at http://journal.sjdm.org/8613/jdm8613.html

Jay, F. 2010. *The Joy of Less, A Minimalist Living Guide: How to Declutter, Organize, and Simplify Your Life*. Anja Press

Jerome K. Jerome. 2004. *Three Men in a Boat: To Say Nothing of the Dog*. Penguin

Kondo, M. 2014. *The Life-Changing Magic of Tidying Up: The Japanese Art of Decluttering and Organizing*, Ten Speed Press

Leonard, A. 2010. *The Story of Stuff: How Our Obsession with Stuff Is Trashing the Planet, Our*

Communities, and Our Health-and a Vision for Change.
Simon and Schuster

Millburn, J., Nicodemus, R. 2011. *Minimalism:
Live a Meaningful Life.* Asymmetrical Press

Moliere. 1998. *Tartuffe and the Bourgeois
Gentleman (Dual-Language) (English and French
Edition).* Dover Publications

ReportLinker: *Management & Marketing
Consultancy: Global Industry Guide.* Available at
http://www.reportlinker.com/p0171922-
summary/Management-Marketing-Consultancy-
Global-Industry-Guide.html

Schor, J. 1999. *The Overspent American: Why We
Want What We Don't Need.* Harper Perennial

Schor, J. 2014. *Born to Buy: The Commercialized Child and the New Consumer Cult.* Scribner

Thoreau, H.D. 2013. *Walden.* Empire Books

"Tidy Desk or Messy Desk? Each Has Its Benefits." August 2013. Available at http://www.psychologicalscience.org/index.php/news/releases/tidy-desk-or-messy-desk-each-has-its-benefits.html

A Guide to Marie Kondo's The Life-Changing
Magic of Tidying Up

42446793R00040

Made in the USA
Lexington, KY
22 June 2015